ALL YOU NEE

ALL YOU NEED IS DYNAMITE

Acid, the Angry Brigade,
and the End of the Sixties

DAVE HASLAM

First published in the UK in 2021 by Cōnfingō Publishing

249 Burton Road, Didsbury, Manchester, M20 2WA
www.confingopublishing.uk

Cover design by Zoë McLean, zoe@confingopublishing.uk

Printed by TJ Books Limited

A CIP catalogue record for this book is available from the British Library

ISBN 978-0-9955966-9-6

2 4 6 8 10 9 7 5 3 1

In memory of

CP Lee
Mike Don
Roger Eagle

In March 1971, several people were gathered around a kitchen table in a communal house in Cannock Street, Moss Side, Manchester, just four hundred yards from Manchester City Football Club's home ground at Maine Road. Together, they were working on a new issue of an underground newspaper called *Mole Express*.

Fourteen months later, some of the people in the house that evening were on trial at the Old Bailey with other alleged members of a left-wing terror cell called the Angry Brigade, who were thought to be responsible for more than a hundred attacks on property over a number of years. The accused were facing charges including conspiracy to carry out two shootings and twenty-three bomb attacks; their targets included the homes of industrialists and Tory cabinet ministers, the American Embassy in London, the Biba boutique, and at least one police station.

The Angry Brigade were also said to be behind the planting of an explosive device in the doorway of the Italian Consulate in Manchester wrapped in a copy of *Rolling Stone* magazine. Fingerprints found at the site of the Manchester bomb were alleged to include those of Anna Mendleson, a recently graduated student from Stockport, and former head girl at Stockport Grammar School for Girls.

There's no trace of the house on Cannock Street now. The street was demolished in 1975 during so-called 'slum clearances' and became part of a new estate. There's also no trace of the Magic Village, which was a basement club and live music venue, from early 1968, at 11 Cromford Court in amongst a host of narrow streets and old pubs dating back to the Victorian era, all buried somewhere under where the Arndale Shopping Centre is now, in the middle of Manchester.

In the years the Magic Village was operating, Manchester's economy was suffering a downturn; industries and trades that had built and sustained the city were falling away, leaving behind empty office buildings and warehouses. There was a darkness in the city centre, arguably metaphorical, but undeniably a physical darkness; smog, smoke-coated buildings, underlit streets, and an increasing number of derelict spaces.

The prime mover behind the Magic Village was Roger Eagle. Previously, Roger had booked the acts at the Twisted Wheel, and been the DJ there. At the Wheel he played rhythm and blues, bluebeat and rare soul, and hosted Manchester shows for the likes of Sonny Boy Williamson, the Spencer Davis Group, and the Yardbirds.

The Twisted Wheel moved in September 1965, from its original home on Brazennose Street to the Piccadilly Station end of Whitworth Street, but Roger Eagle was falling a little out of love with the scene he'd done so much to create. He had a hungry, restless, aficionado's taste in music. He wanted room for adventure, left the Wheel, and developed a new passion – Captain Beefheart and his Magic Band's *Safe as Milk* album.

In August 1967, Scott McKenzie's 'San Francisco (Be Sure to Wear [Some] Flowers in Your Hair)' was number one in the UK charts; it took top spot from 'All You Need Is Love' by the Beatles. But Roger's tastes were more underground. Captain Beefheart was jagged, less soothing than anything representing flower power.

Back at the Twisted Wheel, the scene that was evolving into Northern Soul was fuelled by amphetamines, but in the world Roger was now connected to the drugs of choice were hashish and LSD. It was part of an emerging alternative, already evident in London at film, music, light-show and performance-art 'happenings' at the Roundhouse and all-night events at the UFO Club on Tottenham Court Road; a counterculture of creativity, Soft Machine, Pink Floyd, poetry, radical street theatre, offbeat music, and psychedelic drugs.

Jacko Ogg & the Head People played the first night of the Magic Village, Saturday 9 March 1968. On the second Saturday, Tyrannosaurus Rex headlined, supported by a duo calling themselves Van der Graaf Generator. The duo – Peter Hammill and Chris Judge Smith – were studying at the University of Manchester and living in student accommodation at Owens Park. The show at the Magic Village was only their third (their second, a few weeks previously at a 'happening' at Owens Park, had ended prematurely when the band – on that occasion performing as a three-piece – were bottled off the stage by medical students).

Roger booked a variety of underground, psychedelic, post-blues, and folk acts. There were live performances by the likes of Jethro Tull, Fairport Convention, and the Groundhogs. John Peel favourites the

Liverpool Scene were frequently featured at the Village, as were the Edgar Broughton Band. On Saturday nights, the venue was open from 7 p.m. until 7 or 7.30 in the morning (it was alcohol-free). The Magic Village also went through phases of opening in the afternoons, just to give regulars somewhere to hang out.

One of Roger Eagle's most intriguing concepts was to invite Mike Don to set up a stall selling underground newspapers in the Magic Village every Saturday night. Mike had arrived in Manchester from Edinburgh in 1964 to study at the university. In 1967, he moved into a bedsit at 14 Victoria Grove in Fallowfield, where he encountered Roger Eagle for the first time. He heard some Chicago blues blasting out from a room downstairs. It was just the kind of thing Mike was into, so he knocked on the door, and the two became great friends.

Mike Don's stock of underground newspapers included *Rolling Stone*, *International Times*, and *Oz*, and, a little later, *Friends* (founded in late 1969, and renamed *Frendz* in early 1971). A weekly challenge was to make sure his stall was safe from water dripping through the ceiling in the dark Dickensian cellar. In 1970, Mike would progress from selling underground papers to being a co-founder of *Moul Express*; by March 1971 and the meeting in Cannock

Street, there had been a dozen issues, and it had been renamed *Mole Express*.

The day after that second Saturday at the Village, Mike Don was in London attending a large anti-Vietnam War demo at the American Embassy on Grosvenor Square which attracted twenty-five thousand protesters, and culminated in pitched battles with the police (there were nearly three hundred arrests). Protesters were enraged not just by America's actions in Vietnam, but also by the failure of European governments and political parties to challenge the US. In July 1968, the Nice appeared at the Magic Village just three days after they'd been banned from London's Royal Albert Hall after burning an American flag on stage.

Magic Village regular Nicky Crewe once explained to me she'd often visit the Village during the day, treating it as much as a coffee bar as a music venue.[1] It was an alternative lifestyle, and music mattered, but not only the music: 'It was an intense period of time. People were talking about a lot of things, politics not just music. It was just fascinating and there was nobody telling me I shouldn't be going there or doing that.'

---

[1] I interviewed Nicky Crewe during my research for *Life After Dark: A History of British Nightclubs & Music Venues* (Simon & Schuster, 2015). The book includes more on Roger Eagle.

+

In the short-cut, reductive way we so often sum up decades, the sixties are usually represented by a series of carefree episodes including Merseybeat, mini-skirts, Carnaby Street, flower power, and Woodstock. For sure, young teenagers at the beginning of the 1960s enjoyed freedom from the constrictions faced by the generations that had been trying to make a life through the Second World War and its immediate aftermath, and there were jobs for school leavers but, for many people in Britain, the notion of the Swinging Sixties was something a million miles from daily experience, just a phenomenon they'd read about in tabloid gossip columns. In addition, by the late sixties, there were dark clouds: for one thing, the decline in Manchester's traditional industries led to 50,000 job losses in the manufacturing sector in the city by the end of the decade. In *X-Ray*, his semi-fictional autobiography, Ray Davies of the Kinks insists 'the sixties were a con, the establishment still ruled the country'.[2]

The sixties were also scarred by the reluctance of the authorities in the USA and Britain to accede to demands for racial equality. Black Americans seeking

---

[2] Ray Davies, *X-Ray: The Unauthorized Autobiography* (Overlook Press, 1995), 79.

civil rights in the early 1960s were blessed with the leadership of Dr Martin Luther King. It's worth recalling that in addition to the fearless, articulate optimism he displayed in opposition to segregation, he was also strongly critical of the economic disparities integral to capitalism, and outspoken in his views of the 'abominable evil' of the 'unjust war in Vietnam'. He's now revered, but at the time was widely hated by white America: in a poll just before he was killed, 75 per cent of Americans disapproved of Dr King and his actions.

Faced with an escalation in the war in Vietnam and resistance to progressive ideas, the student movement increasingly contemplated moving beyond reformism and towards direct conflict. Momentum lay less with the soft-focused hippies and more with those advocating major social change by any means necessary. In December 1967, Paul Krassner, Abbie Hoffman and friends became aware of what Krassner called the phenomenon of an 'organic coalition of psychedelic hippies and political activists' and dreamed up a name: the Youth International Party – Yippie for short. The battle was against what one writer called 'the death culture of advanced capitalism'.[3]

---

[3] John Spiers, *The Underground and Alternative Press in Britain* (Harvester Press, 1974), 15.

In the wake of the killing of Dr Martin Luther King in April 1968, a further hardening of attitudes became evident. The Black Panthers offered a more caustic challenge to white America. Concluding that violence had a part to play in self-defence and social change, as one writer puts it, 'the Panthers articulated the rage that King was either unable or unwilling to expose.'[4]

The pushback from the forces of reaction was relentless: two days after Dr King was killed, 17-year-old Black Panther Bobby Hutton was murdered by police in Oakland, California. He had surrendered but they still shot him dead.

In Germany in this period, the Chancellor was a former Nazi party member, Kurt Georg Kiesinger. The murder by German police of a demonstrator, Benno Ohnesorg, and, in April 1968, the attempted assassination of prominent student movement leader Rudi Dutschke by a young anti-communist, Josef Bachmann, was a reflection of a widening gulf between radical groups and the state, exacerbated by the demonisation of protesters by the right-wing media.

---

[4] Mark Anthony Neal, *What the Music Said: Black Popular Music and Black Public Culture* (Routledge, 1999), 58.

The leaders of the straight world – politicians and reactionary newspaper proprietors particularly – painted the challenges to authority of the civil rights activists and the student movement as anarchy, anti-war activity as unpatriotic, and drug use as a mark of moral decline. Feeding, and riding on, these fears, Richard Nixon won the November 1968 election in the USA. The early months of his presidency saw an escalation in Vietnam, and angry desperation among his opponents. In 1969, the Weather Underground emerged out of the American protest group Students for a Democratic Society, embarking on a domestic bombing campaign to create chaos targeting the agents of American imperialism. In their words, 'to bring the war home'.

Empowered by his election victory, Nixon unapologetically abused and suppressed student protests. At Kent State University in Ohio on 4 May 1970, after several days of increasingly tense demonstrations against American foreign policy, Ohio's National Guardsmen opened fire on the crowd, killing four unarmed students. In response, *International Times* declared, 'There will be revolution' and slammed 'Nixon's ultimate orgasm as he kills four students'.[5] The

---

[5] *International Times*, 31 May 1970.

massacre inspired the song 'Ohio' by Crosby, Stills, Nash & Young.

Mole Express covered the massacre at Kent State and featured the Weather Underground more than once. The paper was in no sense parochial: as a bible for Manchester's yippies, freaks, and acid-head lefties, it felt itself connected to the underground's internationalism, and its sense of shared aspirations, style, and attitude. And also its belief that sexual repression was a burden, and – even more of a defining characteristic of the underground – its acceptance, and championing, of the use of drugs.

Leaving the Magic Village at seven in the morning, an entourage including Roger, Dave Backhouse (the in-house light-show operator), Mike, and usually one or two others, would stumble out of the basement and walk up Market Street and through Piccadilly Gardens – not infrequently pursued at walking pace by a police car, says Mike: 'The police assumed the staff at the club would be more likely to have dope on them than the customers were, and then we'd have great difficulty in finding a cab that would take us home because we were a disreputable-looking bunch.'

+

By the middle of 1970, there were two principal underground papers based in Manchester: *Grass Eye* and *Mole Express*. There were fifty-seven issues of *Mole*, until the publication folded in 1977. There was an ever-changing editorial team, with Mike Don as the one common factor. 'A single somewhat bloody-minded individual determinedly keeping the flame' is how he describes himself.

The usual contents of *Mole Express* included information about global political issues and associated local campaigns, music news, drug busts, and community and other activity outside of the cultural and political mainstream. In 1974, in one of the first books to document the underground press in Britain, *Mole* was said to provide 'an exceptional picture of alternative arguments in action in Manchester'.[6]

Mike Don is still in Manchester, but not feted by the civic leadership or the cultural establishment. He never earned any kind of living from producing the paper; through most of the 1970s, he worked at Grass Roots bookshop. Mike tells me Manchester's Central Library received a copy of every edition of *Mole*, but he believes they were destroyed.

There were far fewer issues of *Grass Eye* – it

6 Spiers, *Underground and Alternative Press*, 22.

had ceased publication by 1971 – but in May 1970 *Grass Eye* included a brief article about the cultivation of marijuana from hemp seed. A contributor called Adam reported that hemp seed could be bought in fishing tackle shops (there were a number on Tib Street); the seeds are used as groundbait by anglers. Adam had decided to sow the seeds at the beginning of the previous summer. He harvested his crop in September and then dried and smoked some leaves. 'It did not have the desired effect,' he wrote.

Mike didn't keep many copies of *Mole*, but a few years ago he was gifted a big pile of them, which he then passed on to the Working Class Movement Library in Salford. A more complete collection is held at the University of Brighton Library and with their help Manchester Digital Music Archive have built an online exhibition of back issues of *Mole*.[7]

The radical, trouble-making Edgar Broughton Band were a quintessential Magic Village act, but a range of music reflected the insane times. *Mole* gave major coverage to a radio station called Geronimo broadcasting via the Radio Monte Carlo transmitter from midnight until 3 a.m. three nights a week, with a playlist that turned on the audience to songs even

---

[7] https://www.mdmarchive.co.uk

beyond the eclectic range Roger Eagle programmed at the Magic Village. Presenters would segue music made in Mali into tracks by Soft Machine, Albert Ayler, or Judy Collins. Unfortunately, by the end of November, the station had closed.

When it comes to art and ideas, I'm interested in the nonconformists on the fringes, the margins, the underground. Looking through the pages of *Grass Eye* and *Mole Express*, the determined political engagement is striking, although in retrospect the era was also marked by a raggedness of thought at times, and a fuzzy logic; generally, it feels like a lost chapter, underdocumented. On the face of it, the freaks and the yippies were a generation with few outright and lasting victories; interesting odysseys turning into dead ends, bands breaking up before their first album, political campaigns failing, discarded newspapers, radio stations closing, music venues running out of money.

Punk, which emerged several years later, has been portrayed as a 'year zero' characterised by a dismissive rejection of the past. Undeniably, in 1976, part of the energy and attitudes of the likes of the Sex Pistols came from their antipathy to mid-1970s rock aristocracy, but behind the apparent rejection of what had gone before, the story of punk's relationship to the freak scene is less clear-cut. When John Lydon of the

Pistols guested on Capital Radio in July 1977 to talk about his favourite music, he went out of his way to praise Peter Hammill of Van der Graaf Generator.

An intriguing idea from the margins can live on, and emerge late, and unexpectedly. Seven or eight years ago I was talking to Liz Naylor. Liz grew up in Droylsden which, it's fair to say, isn't renowned for its bohemian subcurrents. Liz told me *Mole Express* was a lifeline to her, a guide to alternative ideas. And that *Mole Express* had been one of the reasons she became involved in writing for and contributing to *City Fun*, a Manchester punk and post-punk fanzine. In turn, the work that Liz did at *City Fun*, with her colleague Cath Carroll, inspired me to write my own fanzine *Debris*.

Ideas disseminated by Mike – dangerously disreputable to some, gloriously disreputable to others – and his personal passion for *Mole* – obvious to all – lived on in the underground, emerging through the cracks, but quietly unstoppable, finding its way through culture, down the decades, like that water finding its way through the cracks between the bricks in the Magic Village.

Demands for change among the freaks, hippies, dropouts and yippies, however, were riven with conspicuous fault lines, as noted in *International Times*: 'There seems to be a division in the underground between those who want to change their heads and those who want to change society.'[8] For customers at Mike Don's stall at the Magic Village, was the answer to be found in the quasi-mystical underground paper *Gandalf's Garden*, or in the pages of *The Black Dwarf*, one of the most hardcore (left-wing) alternative newspapers of the day?

If you figure you're living in an unhappy, unequal and unjust world, how do you survive? What strategies are available to you when existing political structures are irrelevant or even an obstacle to social progress? When the state's antipathy to your attitudes is total? When governments and newspapers feed division? And polite marches and demonstrations are ignored and even reformist and peaceful street protests are suppressed?

+

Opposition to America's involvement in Vietnam led directly to the Paris *événements* of May 1968. On the same weekend as the Grosvenor Square demo in March, a couple of hundred students mostly from the Nanterre campus attacked the American Express

---

[8] *International Times*, 4 May 1972.

offices in Paris (on Rue Scribe, near l'Opéra). Six students were arrested. Then, on 22 March, students took the decision to occupy the faculty lounge in the administration building at Nanterre in support of their arrested comrades.

Some weeks later, on the eve of the disciplinary hearings of students arrested at the American Express demo, police moved into buildings at the Sorbonne in the centre of Paris and began arresting protesters. Battles developed at the university and on the surrounding streets. Students began to light fires, tear up paving stones and build barricades.

Events accelerated over the next few days as students took to the streets and the police responded. There was talk of a general strike, the students looking to make common cause with workers. Radical ideas and open debate were encouraged; it was all high ideals and crazy dreams on the streets. The philosophy of the student activists, according to Sartre, 'expanded the field of the possible'.

Some of the slogans on posters and graffiti appearing in the Latin Quarter of Paris reflected the influence of ideas and phrases propagated by artists and thinkers who were attached to the Situationist International. Situationists believed that capitalism forces us into lives that become chained to the spectacle of consumer society. To disrupt this – and return to freedom and discover our creative human potential – situations must be engineered that reveal (or, better still, destroy) the web of illusions at the heart of power and control. The key texts included Guy Debord's *The Society of the Spectacle* and a work by the Belgian philosopher Raoul Vaneigem whose *Traité de savoir-vivre à l'usage des jeunes générations* (translated as *The Revolution of Everyday Life*) was published shortly before the eruption of student protest in Paris in May '68.

This kind of imaginative, myth-busting anger, hand-in-hand with huge support from workers in key and major industries, was a combination that seemed like it could be unassailable. On 17 May 1968, thousands of students in Paris marched for a second day in a row from the Sorbonne to the Renault plant occupied by its workers to support them. All over France dozens of workplaces were occupied.

Les événements challenged not only the authorities, but also the puritanical, and hierarchical, French Communist Party (the PCF) who dominated the huge and highly controlled labour union, the CGT. According to the anarchist writer Stuart Christie – one of the defendants at the Angry Brigade trial in 1972 – it was ordinary rank and file workers rather than trade union leaders who embraced the idea of joining the students in the struggle: 'Neither of the two major French unions, the CGT and CFDT, were ever on the side of the revolutionaries; they merely used the situation as a bargaining chip in wage negotiations'.[9]

Some of the notions propounded by the Situationists were never going to find favour among labour unions. In Chapter 5 of *The Revolution of Everyday Life* Vaneigem slams 'the cult of work', declaring that both the capitalist and the Soviet economies prioritise productivity over life, killing off sparks of humanity, and creativity. In London, King Mob, a Situationist cell of artists and activists who engaged in disruptive actions of various kinds, challenged what they considered the facile, deadened state of society. 'SAME THING DAY AFTER DAY,' read the graffiti they left along the Hammersmith and City Line. 'TUBE – WORK – DINNER – ARMCHAIR – SLEEP […] HOW MUCH MORE CAN YOU TAKE? – ONE IN TEN GO MAD – ONE IN FIVE CRACKS UP'.

At the end of May, the uprising collapsed. The government agreed emergency wage increases with the unions, and President de Gaulle reasserted his authority by mobilising more than half a million sup-

---

[9] Stuart Christie, *Edward Heath Made Me Angry – the Christie File: Part 3, 1967-1975* (ChristieBooks, 2004), 49.

porters in a march down the Champs-Élysées. In general elections later in the summer, with promises to end anarchy and protect law and order that appealed to citizens more comfortable with the status quo, the Gaullists gained a sizeable majority.

A favourable moment presaging a political and cultural revolution, a glimpse of a moment when the door seemed to have been pushed open by a new generation with ideas beyond the dormant mindset and unimaginative political strategies of the political classes. But the door had shut.

At the end of May 1968, an issue of *International Times* covered the uprising in France alongside an article by Bert Bensen, who had interviewed Rudi Dutschke earlier in the year. Bensen ended the article by pointing out that 'there is a double standard in which state violence is legitimate while popular opposition, especially reactive popular violence, is "unlawful"'. The following year, 1969, as if to underline this, in total twenty-seven Black Panthers were killed.

In Italy in December 1969, a bomb exploded at a bank in Milan killing seventeen people. Suspicion centred on the members of the 22 March Group (named after the student group at Nanterre), including Giuseppe Pinelli, a 41-year-old railroad worker and leading member of the Milan-based anarchist association Ponte della Ghisolfa. Pinelli was taken into custody and interrogated; three days into the interrogation, he fell to his death from the fourth-floor window of the police station. Pinelli's family and his comrades denied he'd any involvement in the bombings, and accused the police of murder. The Italian Anarchist Federation demanded an independent enquiry and affirmed its horror at 'the absurd and bestial massacre in Milan'. Their contention was that the bomb attacks were the work of 'agents-provocateurs in the pay of the organisers of a right-wing putsch'.[10]

What happened in Milan that day in December 1969 would become the pretext for a bomb attack in Manchester. The Summer of Love seemed like ancient history. Another piece of King Mob graffiti scrawled on a wall in London read: 'ALL YOU NEED IS DYNAMITE'.

+

At the beginning of 1970, *International Times* carried news that the Magic Village had closed. The economic reality of struggling to pay rent, wages and fees, and

---

[10] The statement first appeared in the newspaper *Umanità Nova*; a translated version was printed in the anarchist weekly newspaper *Freedom*, 10 January 1970.

continual harassment from the drug squad, made survival impossible. Roger Eagle had in fact left several weeks before the last night, but soon resurfaced booking acts into a Liverpool venue called the Stadium. His first show there, in May 1970, was headlined by the Edgar Broughton Band. The same month, the Edgar Broughton Band were the cover stars of *Zigzag* music magazine (which had been launched the previous year).

After the Magic Village closed, Mike Don continued to sell underground newspapers wherever and whenever he could, but also his involvement deepened. He'd started writing in *Grass Eye* and then became involved in setting up *Moul Express*.

The very first issue of *Moul Express* was published in May 1970, sixteen black and white pages, with a cover price of 2/-. *Grass Eye* was supportive of the new venture, describing it as 'written by and for yippies and acid freaks'.

The first issues of *Moul* engaged with multiple subjects, including education, abortion rights, and the environment. Some coverage was hyper-local, including news that three lads at Stand Grammar School in Whitefield (North Manchester) had been suspended for refusing to cut their hair (one of the boys was called Jim Morrison); Mark E Smith (later of the Fall) was attending the school at the time, but was not implicated in the long-hair scandal.

In addition to a lengthy polemic about the need for more play facilities for young children in Manchester, housing was a major concern in the first few issues of *Mole*, and stayed close to the front of the agenda throughout its publishing history. In 1970, in areas including Moss Side and Hulme, there was determined opposition to local housing development, the 'slum clearances': demolishing Victorian terraced streets, building new estates, and moving families to other districts. The council had denied the local community any meaningful voice when they formulated and delivered their plans. A housing action group was formed by the Moss Side People's Association (MSPA), who launched a small-circulation newspaper, *Moss Side News*.

Issue four of *Moul* included a poem by John Cooper Clarke, possibly the first published work by the poet. In the lifetime of the paper, *Mole Express* published the work of comic-strip creators and cartoonists including Peter Kirkham, Bill Tidy, and Tony Husband.

During the summer of 1970, *Mole* kept readers updated on the goings-on at a venue in Manchester called Mr Smiths, where the team from *Grass Eye* had been running an event they called 'Electric Circus' every Sunday. John Cooper Clarke was one of the performers there on Sunday 19 July 1970. Early issues of *Moul* included articles on Sun Ra, jazz rock, and Mott the Hoople. The most written-about local group in both *Grass Eye* and *Mole Express* were Greasy Bear, an act that had evolved from Jacko Ogg & the Head People and included both CP Lee and Bruce Mitchell in the line-up.

Mole also gave news of DJs around the city who played progressive music; less than a handful, basically. Oceans 11, on Anson Road close to Dickinson Road – a venue that had previously been Birch Park Skating Palace – was recommended on Tuesdays (which were hosted by DJ Chinese Pete). The paper also recommended Auntie's Kitchen on Bow Lane, off Clarence Street. Adverts for weekend nights promised 'Underground Sounds', 'Freak Lights', and 'Exotic Dancers'. The building that housed Auntie's Kitchen is now a branch of the Croma restaurant chain.

Early issues of *Moul* tracked not just the local music news but also the growing number of businesses close to where the Magic Village had operated. The area had become a popular hangout for hippies and freaks. On The Eighth Day opened at 19 New Brown Street on 5 September 1970 when a group of five friends opened the co-operatively run venture, a 'head shop' in the parlance of the time, selling handmade crafts, paintings, coats, dresses, Che Guevara posters, and joss sticks. The building in which On The Eighth Day first operated was demolished to make way for the Arndale shopping centre; but the co-operative is still trading (now at 111 Oxford Road).

Local news shared the pages with many international subjects. Issue 4 included a page devoted to explaining and celebrating the Weather Underground. The Weather Underground are the vanguard, it read: 'the spark that will create the situation that will lead to total revolution'.

Moul writers and readers were disillusioned and impatient with creaky trad-left politics; Issue 3 was published just before the 1970 General Election. According to *Moul*, refusing to vote is the only course to take. The 'election game' is 'an essential part of the Spectacle-in-Society', it said (with more than a nod to Situationist writings). Elections are 'a basic ingredient of the BIG CON', *Moul* continued. Readers were told: 'Vote YIPPIE! Vote for the All-Night Party'.

Later in 1970, Issue 7 of *Mole* carried a second article celebrating the Weather Underground. The organisation had ramped up their activities; for example, within days of the Kent State massacre, having issued a declaration of war, the Weather Underground set off explosions in the offices of Chase Manhattan, Standard Oil, and General Motors. Five hundred and forty-six acts of guerrilla sabotage and terrorism were recorded in the first nine months of 1970 in the USA, compared to only sixteen in the whole of 1965. In June 1970, *International Times* told its readers: 'It's all out war against honky Amerika and if you still need reasons in 1970, you are beyond understanding'.

+

A growth in direct action and violent insurrection by leftist groups wasn't limited to the Weather Underground. In 1970, Italy's far-left terror gang, the Red Brigades, was formed. In Germany, the Red Army Faction, emerging out of the combustible situation that had developed in that country, had instigated a wave of bombings, robberies, and shootings. Their rationale was explained by Stefan Aust in the underground newspaper *Konkret*: 'The moment you see your own country as the continuation of the fascist state, you give yourself permission to do almost anything against it.'

Many of the first actions in Britain were claimed by the First of May Group, activists opposing Franco's fascist regime in Spain. Between August 1967 and February 1969, the group claimed responsibility for machine-gunning the American Embassy in London, bombing the Spanish Embassy in London, and damaging the Bank of Spain in Liverpool. Already active politically and known to the police, Stuart Christie came under suspicion of involvement in these attacks, given his anti-Franco history: he'd served time in a Spanish jail after transporting plastic explosives to a rendezvous at an American Express office in Madrid. Christie had been at the Grosvenor Square demo, and was in regular contact with the likes of Dany Cohn-Bendit, a high-profile figure at Nanterre and in the May '68 *événements*.

Ongoing demands for equal access for the Catholic minority to housing, jobs and voting rights by civil rights campaigners in Northern Ireland were being denied by the Ulster and British governments. In a violent pushback against the Catholic community during the weekend of 14 and 15 August 1969, over a hundred and fifty Catholic homes were burned. That weekend, eight civilians were killed, including four shot by the Royal Ulster Constabulary (one was the first child killed in the Troubles, Patrick Rooney, aged nine).

In a reprisal attack on 17 August, the Ulster Office on Savile Row in London was firebombed.

Ian Purdie was later charged and found guilty of this attack. Purdie had been at Grosvenor Square in 1968, and had then become active in the early days of the Irish civil rights campaign. In February 1970, he was sentenced to nine months, and sent to the Albany prison on the Isle of Wight where he shared a cell with Jake Prescott, a career criminal from a troubled background whose thieving had spun out of control when he began to struggle with heroin addiction. Prescott had been jailed for possession of a gun.

In two other attacks in 1969, a bomb was thrown into an army recruitment office in Brighton, and the home of Tory MP Duncan Sandys was firebombed. In May 1970, a bomb was discovered at the new high-security Paddington police station. The following month, the Brixton Conservative Association was attacked. Around the same time, *Moul Express* was asking a question many local yippies and acid freaks were asking: 'We wonder why no Pig property in Manchester has been touched yet?'

Within months, urban terrorism would arrive in Manchester. On 9 October 1970, in revenge attacks for the death of Giuseppe Pinelli, the Italian Consulate in the city was one of four simultaneous attacks on buildings with Italian government connections (the others were in London, Birmingham, and Paris). Coverage of these incidents was suppressed by the authorities, however (similarly, after attacks on the homes of the Commissioner of the Metropolitan Police Sir John Waldron, and the Attorney General Sir Peter Rawlinson, Scotland Yard issued memos to news editors requesting a media blackout until enquiries were complete).

A device containing four ounces of TNT damaged a BBC van parked outside the Albert Hall in November 1970, the night before a live broadcast of the Miss World contest; this was followed by the bombing of the offices of the Department of Employment and Productivity. Both actions were claimed by the Angry Brigade in communiqués sent to the press. Forensics established that the explosives used in these attacks matched those of the First of May Group attacks.

On 12 January 1971, there were demonstrations against the Industrial Relations Bill which the Tories had introduced to restrict the power of trade unions. That same evening, the house of Robert Carr, Edward Heath's Minister of Employment, was bombed, the action claimed by the Angry Brigade. A communiqué read: 'The Angry Brigade is after Heath now. We're getting closer.'

The government instructed Scotland Yard to ramp up the search for the bombers, Detective Chief

Superintendent Roy Habershon leading the investigation. In addition, the *Daily Mirror* put up a £10,000 reward for information leading to the arrest of the gang (the equivalent of £130,000 today). The Angry Brigade were now being talked about as Public Enemy Number One.

Issue 10 of *Mole Express* reported: 'The electricity sub-station in Altrincham "tampered with" according to the *Manchester Evening News*, was in fact BOMBED, possibly as a practice run by a local liberation group'. The paper seemed to be one step ahead of the authorities: 'Further, the man picked up by police and charged in connection with the incident did not, in fact, have anything to do with it. He just happened to be around.'

Habershon organised raids on homes and premises thought to have connections with the extra-parliamentary left. Raids in January 1971 included one on Cinema Action, a left-wing film collective, and the questioning of Paul Lewis of *International Times*; his office at the paper and his home were searched.

The culture of communes and underground newspapers, and left-wing and anarchist political networks with connections to Spain and Italy, were phenomena the police had little knowledge of (and no instinctive sympathy for). Information from any magazines and letters they found was useful, but addresses were of most value to them; they needed to build a sense of this world and the network. Habershon later described Christie's address book as a 'glossary of revolutionaries'.

The police scored a major breakthrough by accident rather than design when Jake Prescott was picked up and arrested; he was carrying stolen cheque books and a small amount of cannabis resin. Owing to his existing police record, he was placed on remand in Brixton. His cellmates later reported him to the authorities, claiming he'd told them of his involvement in Angry Brigade attacks. Subsequently, after three days of questioning during which Prescott was denied a lawyer, Habershon and his police colleagues believed they had reasons to charge him with the attacks on Carr's home and the BBC van.

The communiqués from the Angry Brigade kept on coming: 'We are being attacked daily,' said Communiqué #6. 'Violence does not only exist in the army, the police and the prisons. It exists in the shoddy alienating culture pushed out by TV films and magazines, it exists in the ugly sterility of urban life. It exists in the daily exploitation of our labour'.

In early March, Purdie was arrested, and then formally charged with conspiring with Jake Prescott 'and others' to cause explosions likely to endanger life. Through 1971, up to and through their trial, they received support from some, but not all, sections of the underground press; of the higher circulation papers, *Frendz* was the most supportive. There were demonstrations held to support the two men, including one on Clapham Common in September; 'Ian and Jake are our moral consciences in the dock – millions share their beliefs and their anger,' *Frendz* wrote at the time.[11]

While Purdie and Prescott were being held awaiting trial, bombings continued, although the target chosen on 1 May 1971 – the Biba boutique – was a choice that alienated some allies. The communiqué issued by the Angry Brigade twisted a line from a Bob Dylan song, while echoing Situationist writings: 'If you're not busy being born you're busy buying,' it read. 'Life is so boring there is nothing to do except spend all our wages on the latest skirt or shirt. Brothers and Sisters, what are your real desires?' During a labour dispute at Ford's, the home of Ford's managing director, William Batty, and a transformer at its Dagenham factory were both attacked.

On 30 November 1971, Prescott was convicted of conspiring to cause explosions and sentenced to fif-

---

[11] *Frendz*, 16 September 1971.

teen years' imprisonment; Purdie, however, was acquitted. By the end of the year, ten other young people were facing charges and a court case. Six of the ten were arrested in August 1971 when the police raided 359 Amhurst Road in Stoke Newington and arrested Jim Greenfield, Anna Mendleson, John Barker, and Hilary Creek, and picked up Stuart Christie and Chris Bott the next day when they called separately at the flat.

+

There were ten defendants at the pre-trial hearing in the first week of January 1972, but proceedings against two were dropped. The remaining eight – the six picked up at the house on Amhurst Road in August and two others – Kate McLean and Angela Weir – were all charged with conspiring to cause explosions in Britain likely to endanger life or cause serious injury to property; they became known as the Stoke Newington Eight. Other charges against some of the accused included attempts to cause explosions, possession of explosive substances, firearms and ammunition, and the handling of a stolen car. The accused pleaded not guilty to all the charges.

When the trial began on 30 May 1972, John Mathew, prosecuting, explained that the explosions were 'aimed at the property of those they considered to be their political opponents'. That the targets were property and measures were taken to avoid injuring people was a point that the Angry Brigade often made; the group didn't pursue their aims with the brutality of other terrorist organisations.

On 6 December, at the close of what at the time was the longest and costliest trial ever at the Old Bailey, Anna Mendleson, Hilary Creek, John Barker, and James Greenfield were each jailed for ten years. Chris Bott had been found not guilty on four counts earlier in the trial. Stuart Christie was also acquitted; it was generally accepted during the trial that some evidence against him had been planted in the boot of his car by police. Mike Don suggests the police were 'very very upset' not to have secured Christie's conviction.

Even having put eight people in the dock, the police acknowledged that it was unlikely that those who'd been on trial were the Angry Brigade's only members (while five of the defendants were on remand in prison awaiting trial, and the others were under house arrest, a dozen or more attacks took place, including an attempt to blow up the Post Office Tower in London). The police probed a hundred and twenty incidents between March 1968 and August 1971 when homemade bombs caused explosions or were discovered and made safe or failed to explode. They focused on just twenty-five of the incidents which they claimed had enough factors in common to suggest that the same cell was responsible.[12]

An issue of *Mole Express* published in June 1972 included two pages about the ongoing trial and a centrefold pull-out poster expressing solidarity with the Stoke Newington Eight. The campaign on their behalf was very active, producing information, and posters, and arranging rallies. Campaign material spread the word on police lies, and the ideologies of the alleged bombers. One leaflet linked the Miss World and the Biba attacks, both targets, it said, representing 'the most exploitative area of the consumer society – that which sells women, which insults women both in the eyes of others and in their own eyes, and makes a profit from it.[13]

During the trial, attention turned to the bomb at the Italian Consulate in Manchester in October 1970; the Consulate was on Brown Street, close to Manchester's main post office (and to the back entrance of a popular nightclub called Rowntree's). The prosecution

---

[12] For more details of the Angry Brigade, their actions and the trial of the Stoke Newington Eight, see Gordon Carr, *The Angry Brigade: A History of Britain's First Urban Guerilla Group* (PM Press, 2010).

[13] http://thesparrowsnest.org.uk/collections/public_archive/PAR0337_b.pdf

reported forensics had found fourteen sets of fingerprints on the copy of *Rolling Stone* that was in the
bag along with the bomb. Although the fingerprints
of Anna Mendleson and Jim Greenfield were among
those, presenting her own defence Anna told the court
they were in Wivenhoe (near Essex University), and
had witnesses who could corroborate their alibis. She
also pointed out that it wasn't surprising the magazine had passed through many hands given the nature
of communal life. There was also discrepancy in the
evidence, as some Manchester police officers couldn't
even recall seeing the magazine on the crime scene.

Mike Don had recognised the names Hil-
ary Creek, John Barker, and Chris Bott when he read
about the Amhurst Road arrests. He'd met them in
Manchester. He'd been to their house on Cannock
Street, where together they had written, typed up and
laid out *Mole Express*. 'They had much the same sort of
politics as me, which is basically libertarian, socialist,
anarchist,' he says. 'Their politics was fairly radical but
they never gave any impression of being involved in
planting bombs and so on.'

I guess the way they were being portrayed in
the press was extreme anyway, but you found it very
difficult to square with what you knew of them per-
sonally?

'Yeah, they were my sort; I got on with them. There were quite a few people in Manchester like myself who were quite shocked, and running scared for a bit.'

Scared that the state was coming for you, right?

'Because we knew and suspected that the state would be quite capable of doctoring evidence to prove that you were a sinister bomb-throwing anarchist.'

+

Mole #23, published just as the Angry Brigade trial opened, included profiles of the defendants. John Barker had won a scholarship to Clare College, Cambridge. There he took an interest in Situationist writings, although he wasn't ever a signed-up member of the Kim Philby Dining Club, a favourite of the students in thrall to the Situationists and named after the notorious spy who defected to Russia. Barker was involved in sit-ins, disruptions of lectures, and led a campaign against assessment which culminated in him ripping up his final exam papers.

In London he pursued an interest in radical theatre groups, ran a bookstall with Jim Greenfield and lived for a while in 25 Powis Square, a house that features in Nic Roeg and Donald Cammell's film *Perfor-*

mance. With comrades, all wearing suits, he attended an auction of two houses owned by Kensington and Chelsea Council to the private sector, and began to bid up the homes to unreal prices, causing chaos and the collapse of the proceedings.

During one of the Covid-related lockdowns I called up John Barker – now living abroad – and asked him specifically about his months in Manchester, first trying to pin down when he arrived in the city with Hilary Creek. 'As I remember it,' he says, 'it would have been late in 1970, right? Maybe September or October; I don't exactly remember. My partner Hilary had some money and we were able to buy 14 Cannock Street for £400.'

Acres of terraced housing had been demolished in Moss Side and nearby Hulme and the slum clearances were ongoing. 'I think there was some ambiguity about whether the house was going to get knocked down,' he recalls. 'We were aware there were plans. I think there was some kind of guarantee in that case that you would be rehoused.'

The people who moved into the house included a couple with a small child. John describes the residents as a 'mixed bunch of people' and denies my suggestion that the move was partly to dodge police in London looking for members of the Angry Brigade.

The move to Manchester was for 'semi-ideological' reasons perhaps even tinged with a little romanticism, he says. They wanted 'a feeling of being somewhere other than London. We needed to see the world somewhere else, and there were a few of us. And the possibility of having a house so cheap was obviously very attractive.'

The dates are not clear, but whether or not they were in the house by October 1970 and the bombing of the Italian Consulate, John says his arrival in the city and that action were unconnected: 'I'd just arrived in Manchester. You know, a lot of the things from my past are pretty stupid, but I wasn't so stupid that having just moved to Manchester, and probably sticking out, that I would then attack the Italian Consulate in the city.'

Stuart Christie later wrote that 'some of the people on trial had indeed taken part in Angry Brigade actions' while 'some had not'.[14] There are few on-the-record details of who took part in any specific acts, although Jake Prescott wrote to Robert Carr apologising for the attack on his house (an apology Carr accepted), and John Barker, scornful of tactics used against him, has stated that in his case 'the police framed a guilty man'.[15]

---

[14] David Edgar, *London Review of Books*, 16 December 2004.
[15] Gordon Carr, *Angry Brigade*, 180.

During our Zoom call, Barker also implied his involvement in at least one of the actions, describing the bombing of an army recruitment centre on Holloway Road, London on 15 August 1971: 'the last action before our arrest'. However, he wasn't able to recall the circumstances surrounding the attack on the sub-station in Altrincham.

Although the rhetoric of the underground papers and the language of the communiqués could be overblown or fanciful, John and his comrades in Cannock Street, and Mike Don at *Mole*, were all committed to practical action that benefitted their communities. Issue 2 of *Moul* devoted three pages to the work of the local Claimants Union based on Boland Street in Fallowfield, a group dedicated to helping single mothers, the unemployed, strikers, and disabled people to access the benefits they were entitled to. A few months on, and *Mole* in another issue included an anonymous piece likely to have been authored by Hilary Creek about the Claimants Union defending unsupported mothers, who were being harassed by the authorities trying to prove that they cohabited. Chris Bott, John Barker and Hilary Creek all worked together in the Claimants Union in Manchester. 'I don't feel particularly pleased about my past,' says John. 'It's one of the very few things I feel pleased about; the Claimants Union was a terrific organisation.'

Exercising your rights to benefit payments was far from easy then, but there's even more bureaucracy and control, isn't there?

'New Labour filled in a lot of the cracks and now these bastards, I mean, they're really filling in even more cracks and it's very... I think it's very difficult, it's so much tougher to be young now.'

There's a photograph of John Barker, Hilary Creek, Kate McLean, and Chris Bott in Manchester on 12 January 1971 attending a demo against the Industrial Relations Bill, just a few hours before the attack on Robert Carr's house. John says he perceived the Industrial Relations Bill as a first step: 'We had a sense that things were about to change, that capitalism or whatever had had enough. '68 had happened and they said, right, we're not having any more of this. And that in Britain, the starting point would be an attack on the organised working class.'

'I loved Cannock Street, the terraced houses, close together,' volunteers John. 'We got on amazingly well with our neighbours,' he says. He remembers drinking in the Robin Hood pub on Upper Lloyd Street, and calling in on the Asian-owned corner shop at the end of Cannock Street that sold cheap wine. I told him I'd looked through the *Mole Express* events listings pages (which were entitled 'The Spectacle') and during the time he was in Manchester, Soft Machine played at the Free Trade Hall. This was late news to him: 'Regrettably I missed it. If I'd known I would have gone.' He was keen to stress that his abiding memories of being in Manchester were trips to see Manchester City: 'The era of Colin Bell. They were fabulous to watch.'

In the underground press of the time, it's clear drugs are such an important issue. I mentioned to John that I was aware he was enthusiastic about LSD at this point.

'Acid, yes, because you felt the world to be, you know, one of subatomic particles and actually underneath the woodwork, it was all about energy because you could feel it physically. It's very physical; I've walked a lot on acid actually, because it's really high energy. Acid can also be very cartoonish.'

It was giving you a perspective that made authority seem ludicrous?

'You see the official world in a very cartoonish way. You would see even a photograph of an authority figure with gravitas and any gravitas just fell away and you kind of thought, well, under the skin, you're not serious at all. I mean this is both true and not true, unfortunately, because of course they are serious bastards.'

While in the North-West, Barker, Mendleson, and Creek were prime movers behind the launch of a paper called *Strike* which John has memory of getting printed at Keele University. It seems also that at one point John and Hilary journeyed over to Liverpool for some kind of underground print fair or conference.

We talked a little about the trauma of communities being broken up by the clearance and redevelopment of Moss Side and Hulme. The residents had no say and no choice. People got moved into new homes, sometimes in other neighbourhoods, or in the new estate in the deck-access housing in adjacent Hulme (including the notorious Crescents). As John says of Hulme: 'Some years later it was then perceived to be a disaster, the way that they redeveloped it and the effect on crime and all the rest of it. I mean it was all incredibly predictable I think. From day one they were having problems.'

It was via the arrest of Jake Prescott that Habershon tracked down the residents of 14 Cannock Street. When Prescott had admitted possession of stolen cheque books under questioning by Habershon he also confirmed he had used one of them to buy return tickets to Manchester the day after the Robert Carr bomb. He also used a stolen cheque to buy food, drink, clothes, and toys for people living in a house in Moss Side, although Prescott said he wasn't able to recall the address.

Detectives pressed him on the Angry Brigade connection. He referred to meeting several people in the Manchester house, naming several (by first name only), including Kay, Hilary, Joe, Chris, and John. It was as a result of trawling through his address book that police found details of the Moss Side house, 14 Cannock Street

The following day, 13 February 1971, Manchester police raided Cannock Street. John says that the atmosphere of the house changed after that raid. He recalls one particular cop by the name of Carmichael who he says was 'a nasty piece of work'. He has talked of a second raid, then a series of unofficial visits: 'It would be dramatic to say that we felt in a state of siege, but it was certainly a feeling that the house wasn't our own any more. We had the feeling that we could be raided at any time, taken in at any time, questioned at any time and in fact the feeling that we would get more and more aggravation from the Manchester police.'[16]

Carmichael had John arrested on a charge of stealing a typewriter from the University of Essex:

---

[16] Gordon Carr, *Angry Brigade*, 75.

'pathetic stuff' is how he describes it. He feared a stitch-up but, to John's amazement, the magistrate threw the whole thing out. John, however, reckoned Carmichael was going to get him one way or another, and that Manchester Special Branch were being directed by people higher up to get some kind of result.

It was time to decamp from Moss Side. The people at 14 Cannock Street who were unconnected with anything that was happening with regard to the Angry Brigade were getting caught up in this police attention: 'I thought all this is unfair on them actually, so me and Hilary called it a day went back to London.'

The final raid on the Cannock Street house was on 26 April. John and Hilary left soon after, but not before some final contributions to *Mole Express*, including an article about the Prescott and Purdie trial accusing the police of illegally seizing property, and holding people without access to lawyers, in order to make a case against them which was – despite all public denials – politically motivated. 'When the Angry Brigade attacked Carr's house, the facts about the series of actions against the bosses couldn't be hushed up,' according to *Mole*. 'The illusion of social peace was shattered. It became absolutely necessary for the

State to show that this sort of "crime" does not pay. Someone has to be put inside for it.'[17]

I asked John to explain the thought process that would take that step from working with the Claimants Union, or being committed to progress women's liberation, anti-apartheid action, and community campaigns, to then target banks, and the homes of industrialists and cabinet ministers: in other words, to sourcing and using dynamite?

'It's about responsibility, which I still believe in now; that powerful people make decisions which affect the lives of thousands of other people with absolutely no consequences to themselves. People in power were making decisions which fucked up lives of other people; and the whole thing was, well, it's going to have consequences.'

In terms of violent direct action, could you make a case for it now, in a similar manner to the bombing of property by the Angry Brigade?

'To do things I was supposed to have done would be suicidal and stupid in the present climate.'

Why do you say that?

'Because of surveillance, technology, cameras and so on and so forth; technically it's far more diffi-

---

[17] *Mole Express*, May 1971.

cult and – although maybe this could change actually – but up until recently the war on terror, the whole notion of the terrorist, and the bomber and so on; it would only be to the benefit of power.'

We discussed the notion that the ruling class will use bomb outrages to strengthen its control and power knowing that this was what motivated the Milan bombings in 1969; the bombings that Pinelli had been arrested for turned out to be the work of far-right agents provocateurs just as Pinelli's anarchist comrades had always said. The outrage gave those in power the fuel to intensify repression of the left-wing opposition. We also talked about the following years, the Red Brigades infiltrated by the police.

'The Red Brigade was infiltrated from day one as far as I can tell,' says John.

To go from the dreams of '68 to Thatcher in eleven years is shocking, isn't it? Perhaps even by the end of your trial, 1972, 1973, the space to dream looked like it had been shut down, the political and economic climate just wasn't conducive to utopianism, as the oil crises hit, the IMF intervened, and unemployment rose.

'From around 1975 onwards, I thought I would be getting out of prison into a period of defeat. I definitely felt that,' says John. But he reminded me that the late 1970s were also a period with activity and action that held great promise; he mentions experiments in communal living, and advances by the women's movement. 'There was still a strong culture of resistance,' he says.

I mentioned Rock Against Racism as another example. John tells me he returned to Manchester in 1978, around two months after he was released. A friend of his from prison was living in William Kent Crescent in Hulme, and together they went to a Rock Against Racism gig in Alexandra Park which was headlined by Buzzcocks and Steel Pulse. 'It blew my mind,' says John. 'This is wow! This is much better. I knew on the other hand that on the big global level we were in retreat, capital's counteroffensive was strong, but that moment in Alexandra Park: wow!'

+

From despair to where? Disengagement from the notion of social revolution wasn't total but the underground's sense of unity and common cause splintered. Some people just wanted to move on, or to settle down, or just get stoned. In March 1972, *Frendz* published a letter from Paul Easton of Newcastle-upon-Tyne complaining that the newspaper's coverage of political issues is 'depressing': 'most of us have an even greater love for filth, debauchery, rock and roll, and dope.'[18]

Mole Express was unrepentant; the political coverage, if anything, increased. Mike was on a mission; there were campaigns to pursue and corruption to be uncovered. The back page of *Mole #15* in August 1971 asked questions of Scotland Yard's Drug Squad, in relation to drug busts and drug trials. The next month *Frendz* mentioned the police's connection to Soho porn dealers: 'We all know corruption and bribery are part of the lawman's wage packet,' the paper wrote.[19]

Through the first half of the 1970s, the moral arbiters who had slammed the long hairs, the Left, the yippies, the subversives, the dope heads, were revealed to be undemocratic, corrupt, and willing to engage in violence. Six months on, in the same issue as the letter from young Mr Easton, *Frendz* announced news of a police corruption trial which had led to two Scotland Yard detectives being found guilty of bribery, corruption, and conspiracy to pervert the course of justice. At the time, there were around seventy officers suspended from duty and thirteen facing criminal charges. By the end of the year, four hundred and

---

18 *Frendz*, 31 March 1972.
19 Ibid., 19 September 1971.

fifty Scotland Yard officers had left the force after disciplinary proceedings. In June 1974, Kevin Gately, a 20-year-old university student, was killed at a protest against the fascist National Front in Red Lion Square, London by a blow to the head, most probably a police baton wielded by a policeman on horseback.

There is much evidence that elements of the Right and the British establishment were considering a military coup to oust Labour's Harold Wilson at the end of the sixties and again from 1974 after he'd defeated Edward Heath in a General Election (one of the characters behind this activity is said to have been newspaper magnate, and a director of the Bank of England, Cecil King). There were also attempts to destabilise Wilson's government by the security services. Through the 1970s and 1980s in Northern Ireland, collusion between the British security services and loyalist paramilitary forces resulted in dozens of deaths.

Reflecting the splintering of the underground, the circulation of the leading underground papers dropped. *Frendz* ceased publication in August 1972. By the end of 1972, issues of *International Times* were selling around 15,000 copies, down from a high of 40,000. In addition, alternative and underground ideas were annexed by the marketplace; in our conversation, John Barker expressed particular disappointment with *Time Out*, which he characterised as 'consumerist'.

On the other hand, there was also evidence that print media still had a role in spreading ideas and information beyond what the powerful mainstream publications provided, and with more focus and understanding than the big names in the underground press had sometimes shown. *Gay News* was founded in June 1972, the same month as the first publication of the feminist magazine *Spare Rib*.

Spare Rib was welcome and necessary. *Mole Express* had been all too aware that the underground was unable to deal with women's liberation. As early as October 1970, the paper reprinted a piece that had first appeared in *RAT*, an underground newspaper based in New York: 'Many problems remain. Male chauvinism still exists in all of us, but we realise that if we are to survive and build for the future macho will have to be smashed.' In May 1971, Hilary Creek and Anna Mendleson had both contributed to a special Women's Issue of *Frendz*, which inspired a series of meetings that led to the founding of *Spare Rib*.[20]

---

[20] Creek and Mendleson's work at *Frendz* discussed by Rosie Boycott in Stuart Christie, *Edward Heath Made Me Angry*, 244.

Looking through back issues of *International Times*, *Frendz*, and *Mole Express*, an unsympathetic reader could find some daft ideas and more than a reasonable amount of hysterical politics, but it's also clear that among their dreams, schemes and wayward attitudes, fifty years ago in so many ways the freaks were ahead of the curve: an awareness and concern for homelessness; information about the side-effects of drugs; leadership in community action against housing redevelopment; fearless coverage of mental health, town hall corruption, gay liberation, and anti-apartheid (and other campaigns for racial equality); and an embrace of ecology and environmental issues.

After being released on parole in 1976, Anna Mendleson spent some time in Stockport and Sheffield before moving to Cambridge where she published poetry under the name Grace Lake; she died in 2009. Angela Weir, one of the Stoke Newington Eight who was acquitted, later became a director of Stonewall and was awarded an OBE. In 2002, BBC Radio 4 broadcast a play about the Angry Brigade trial; Tom Hiddleston played John Barker.

Just before he died in 2006, Tony Ogden, former singer with World of Twist, demoed a song with the lyrics 'I'm gonna go back in time / And join the Angry Brigade'. In 2014, Thurston Moore of Sonic

Youth released 'Grace Lake' on his solo album *The Best Day*, a song inspired by Anna Mendleson's story.

Tony Wilson's years at Cambridge University overlapped John Barker's by a year. In 1996, Wilson hosted a two-day conference discussing 'The Legacy of the Situationist Revolt' at the club he co-owned, the Haçienda, in Manchester.

CP Lee and Bruce Mitchell of Greasy Bear both later featured in the band Alberto y Lost Trios Paranoias. In 1981, Bruce Mitchell took up his place as drummer with Durutti Column.

Roger Eagle left the Stadium in Liverpool and moved on to co-create Eric's, a club and live music venue notable for its influence on the likes of Bill Drummond and Jayne Casey, and the spiritual home of a generation of Liverpool bands including Echo & the Bunnymen, the Teardrop Explodes, and Wah! Heat. Roger went on to work at the International in Manchester, the venue formerly known as Oceans 11 (where DJ Chinese Pete had hosted Tuesdays back in 1970). Roger booked the acts at the International, including, on one occasion, Peter Hammill.[21] Roger Eagle died in 1999. Neither he nor Mike Don lived a life in the lap of luxury; at one point, just after Eric's

---

[21] Peter Hammill at the International, 17 April 1989.

closed, Roger had lived in a warehouse in Liverpool, 'skint to an astonishing degree', according to Bruce Mitchell.[22]

Two weeks before I planned to complete this book, I got news that Mike had died. A neighbour of his called me and invited me to say some words at the funeral. I could have spent some time going back through this book turning 'is' to 'was' but I chose not to. I have left him in the present tense. As if he hasn't left us.

Two dozen mourners gathered at Manchester Crematorium. I began by mentioning what Liz Naylor has said about *Mole Express*, and then recounted a story I'd heard from Bruce Mitchell, that Jacko Ogg & the Head People liked to dress up onstage (Bruce was known to wear a gorilla suit) and even though Mike Don wasn't in the band, he joined in the fun, usually dressed as the Incredible Hulk. It was hard to imagine, but, as Sartre tells us, revolutionaries in that era were expanding the field of possible.

There's a phrase everyone seems to be using now: 'It is what it is.' It's a kind of acceptance. People say it a lot: 'It is what it is.' But some people aren't

---

[22] Bill Sykes, *Sit Down! Listen to This! The Roger Eagle Story* (Empire Publications, 2012), 221.

content with that description of the world, or resigned to the circumstances we're given. People like Mike. Not for him, 'It is what it is' – for him, 'It's not what it could be.'

It took idealism to do what he did with *Mole Express*. An idealism under threat always, of course, from other -isms like cynicism and capitalism. He was one of those priceless characters in every generation that push things on, maybe bend the edges of the culture a little.

Leaving the event, I exchanged a few words with the writer and critic Bob Dickinson who authored *Imprinting the Sticks: The Alternative Press Beyond London* and told him I was close to finishing *All You Need is Dynamite*. I knew the subject was niche but I couldn't deal with the thought that the passions and the ideas of the people I was writing about would be erased in the same way as the Magic Village had been, and the Hulme and Moss Side communities of the sixties and seventies, and Cannock Street. It's uncomfortable history, we agreed, but that's OK; history is an argument not a story, and the conflicts and the challenges are part of it.

I told Bob the book was nearly written, that there were so many things I wish I'd room to include, but at least I knew I had a final quote, from a letter by

Kim Wagner, Professor of Global and Imperial History at Queen Mary University of London, which I'd read in the *London Review of Books*: 'We are not responsible for the past, but we are responsible for what we choose to remember and what we choose to forget.'[23]

---

[23] *London Review of Books*, 18 April 2019.

ORIGINAL ILLUSTRATION & COVER DESIGN

Zoë McLean, Manchester

zoe@confingopublishing.uk

TYPESETTING

John Oakey, Penrith

johnoakey1@gmail.com

BODY TYPE

Minion 3, an updated and expanded version of Robert Slimbach's early 90s design for Adobe.

COVER TYPE

Futura PT, developed at ParaType in 1995 by Vladimir Yefimov, expands on the classic geometric sans-serif typeface Futura designed by Paul Renner in 1927.

OTHER BOOKS BY CŌNFINGŌ PUBLISHING

Ornithology: Sixteen Short Stories Nicholas Royle

We Were Strangers: Stories Inspired by Unknown Pleasures (ed. Richard V. Hirst)

Pharricide Vincent de Swarte (translated by Nicholas Royle)

Between Tongues Paul McQuade

CŌNFINGŌ

confingopublishing.uk